W9-BMO-970

The Declaration of Independence

by Laura K. Murray

First Facts®

The Declaration of Independence

by Laura K. Murray

PEBBLE
a capstone imprint

First Facts are published by Pebble
1710 Roe Crest Drive, North Mankato, Minnesota 56003.
www.mycapstone.com

Library of Congress Cataloging-in-Publication Data
Names: Murray, Laura K., 1989- author.
Title: The Declaration of Independence / by Laura K. Murray.
Description: First edition. | North Mankato, Minnesota : Capstone, an imprint
of Pebble, [2020] | Series: First facts. Shaping the United States of
America | Audience: Grades K–3. | Audience: Ages 6–8.
Identifiers: LCCN 2019004125| ISBN 9781977108425 (hardcover)
ISBN 9781977110114 (pbk.) | ISBN 9781977108609 (ebook pdf)
Subjects: LCSH: United States. Declaration of Independence—Juvenile
literature. | United States—Politics and government—1775–1783—
Juvenile literature.
Classification: LCC E221 .M87 2020 | DDC 973.3/13—dc23
LC record available at https://lccn.loc.gov/2019004125

Editorial Credits
Alesha Sullivan, editor; Elyse White, designer; Jo Miller, media researcher;
Katy LaVigne, production specialist

Photo Credits
Alamy: JG Photography, 9, Kumar Sriskandan, 16, North Wind Picture Archives, 7; Library of
Congress, Prints & Photographs Division, Theodor Horydczak Collection, Cover (bottom); National
Archives Museum, 17; Newscom: akg-images, 13, Picture History, 8, ZUMA Press/Tracy Barbutes, 21;
Shutterstock: Charles Brutlag, 5, Rena Schild, 18; Wikimedia: Historical Society of Pennsylvania, 12,
Library of Congress Prints and Photographs, 14, NARA, 15, United States Government, Cover (top), 11

Design Elements
Shutterstock: Scisetti Alfio

All internet sites appearing in back matter were available and accurate
when this book was sent to press.

Table of Contents

Chapter 1

A Free Nation

In the late 1700s, the American **colonies** decided they wanted to be free from Great Britain's rule. They wanted to be **independent**.

The **Declaration** of Independence was the first step to end Great Britain's control over the colonies. The declaration was adopted on July 4, 1776. This date is known as Independence Day.

In CONGRESS, JULY 4, 1776.

The unanimous Declaration of the thirteen united States of America.

colony—an area that has been settled by people from another country, typically ruled by another country

declaration—an important announcement

independent—free from the control of other people or things

Fighting for Independence

Great Britain ruled the colonies in the **New World**. The colonists had to follow British laws and pay high **taxes**. They weren't allowed to play a part in making or changing any rules. They were being treated unfairly and were unhappy with the British **government**.

King George III did not want to listen to the colonists. In 1775 war broke out between the colonies and Great Britain. The Revolutionary War (1775–1783) had begun.

The Revolutionary War was fought between the American colonies and Great Britain.

government—the group of people who make laws, rules, and decisions for a country or state

New World—the name given to the Americas as they were being explored and settled

tax—money that people or businesses must give to the government to pay for what the government does

Thomas Jefferson wrote the Declaration of Independence with help from other leaders in the Continental Congress.

The colonists wanted to make their own rules. A group of **delegates** from each colony created their own government. The group was called the **Continental Congress**.

On July 2, 1776, delegates agreed to cut ties with Great Britain. Thomas Jefferson wrote a document called the Declaration of Independence. Congress approved the declaration on July 4, 1776, at the Pennsylvania State House.

Continental Congress—a group of people who made important decisions for the colonies and, later, for the United States

delegate—a person who is chosen to act for others; a representative

9

Chapter 3

Powerful Words

The first part of the Declaration of Independence is called the Preamble, or introduction. It says that everyone is created equal. Everyone has the **right** to "life, **liberty**, and the pursuit of happiness."

The middle part describes Great Britain's unfair rules for the colonists. The American people declared their independence at the end of the document.

IN CONGRESS. JULY 4, 1776.

he unanimous Declaration of the thirteen united States of America

the Declaration of Independence

liberty—being able to choose your own way of life

right—something the law allows people to do, such as the right to vote or the right to speak freely

Delegates had to sign the Declaration of Independence before it could become official.

Fifty-six delegates signed the Declaration of Independence. John Hancock was the first. He was president of the Continental Congress. Most in Congress did not sign right away. Some names were kept secret. It was dangerous to be against the British government.

News of the declaration spread quickly. The colonists celebrated. In New York a crowd knocked down a giant **statue** of King George III.

statue—a model of a person made from metal, stone, or wood

The Declaration of Independence helped Americans in the Revolutionary War. They kept the document in mind through hard times. They would not give up the fight for independence. After eight years, the Americans won the war. The colonies were now the United States of America.

Dunlap Broadsides

John Dunlap was a printer who made the first copies of the Declaration of Independence in Philadelphia. The copies are called Dunlap Broadsides. Only 26 copies are known to exist today. In 1989, one was found hidden in a picture frame in Pennsylvania and later sold for $8 million.

After eight years of war, the Americans celebrated their victory over the British in 1783.

Chapter 4

A Lasting Document

Today the Declaration of Independence is located at the National Archives Museum in Washington, D.C. It sits safely inside a special case. The case is strong enough to stay standing even if the building were to fall down.

Staff at the National Archives Museum watch over the Declaration of Independence.

DECLARATION
OF
INDEPENDENCE

17

The Declaration of Independence inspires people to stand up for their rights.

The Declaration of Independence still helps shape America today. People have rights, and the government has rules to follow.

The declaration is important to others around the world too. It gives hope for people's rights.

Every Fourth of July, Americans celebrate Independence Day. We look back at the ways the Declaration of Independence helped shape our country. We remember the birth of America's independence and the freedoms we now enjoy.

Fact:

Independence Day became a national holiday in 1870.

Many cities around the country observe Independence Day with parades and fireworks.

Glossary

colony (KAH-luh-nee)—an area that has been settled by people from another country, typically ruled by another country

Continental Congress (kahn-tuh-nen-tuhl KAHNG-gruhs)—a group of people who made important decisions for the colonies and, later, for the United States

declaration (dek-luh-RAY-shuhn)—an important announcement

delegate (DEL-uh-guht)—a person who is chosen to act for others; a representative

government (GUHV-urn-muhnt)—the group of people who make laws, rules, and decisions for a country or state

independent (in-di-PEN-duhnt)—free from the control of other people or things

liberty (LIB-er-tee)—being able to choose your own way of life

New World (NOO WURLD)—the name given to the Americas as they were being explored and settled in the 1600s

right (RITE)—something the law allows people to do, such as the right to vote or the right to speak freely

statue (STACH-oo)—a model of a person made from metal, stone, or wood

tax (TAKS)—money that people or businesses must give to the government to pay for what the government does

Read More

Betti, Matthew. *The Declaration of Independence and the Continental Congress.* Spotlight on American History. New York: PowerKids Press, 2015.

Clay, Kathryn. *The Declaration of Independence.* Introducing Primary Sources. North Mankato, MN: Capstone, 2018.

Donaghey, Reese. *The History of Independence Day.* What You Didn't Know About History. New York: Gareth Stevens, 2015.

Internet Sites

Ben's Guide to the U.S. Government: The Declaration of Independence
https://bensguide.gpo.gov/declaration-of-independence-1776

The Declaration of Independence: What Does it Say?
https://www.archives.gov/founding-docs/declaration/what-does-it-say

Critical Thinking Questions

1. What important events led to the signing of the Declaration of Independence on July 4, 1776?

2. What do you think might have happened if the colonies stayed under British rule?

3. Do you think the Declaration of Independence is still important today? Explain your answer.

Index